GOSSIP

A One-Act Play

ROBERT SHEPPARD

Jasper Publishing Ltd

115 Harlestone Road, Northampton NN5 7AQ
Tel: 01604 590315 Fax: 01604 591077
jasperpublishing@ukbusiness.com

Jasper Publishing Ltd
115 Harlestone Road, Northampton
NN5 7AQ
Tel: 01604 590315 Fax: 01604 591077

A licence must be obtained prior to any performance, and all fees are payable in advance.

ISBN 1 874009 59 7

British Library Cataloguing-in-Publication Data.
A catalogue record for this book is available from
The British Library

CHARACTERS

Natasha
Mel
Danielle
Ann
Tara
Neil
Claire
Daisy
Jamie
Amy
Alex
Lydia

Time: the present

The action is continuous

'Best original play'
Woking Drama Festival 1998

Also available from **Robert Sheppard** in this series

Dame Agatha's Greatest Case

GOSSIP

A bare stage or rehearsal room. Dramatic lighting reveals the ball scene from 'Romeo and Juliet' in progress. Music plays in the background, masked guests dressed in black and white move or dance around; Capulet and his cousin move forward in conversation

NATASHA	Nay sit, nay sit, good cousin Capulet,
	For you and I are past our dancing days:
	How long is't now since last yourself and I
	Were in a mask?
MEL	Thirty years.
NATASHA	What, man, 'tis not so much, 'tis not so much;
	Some five and twenty years, and then we masked.
MEL	'Tis more, 'tis more.

They move aside as Romeo calls to a servant, indicating offstage

DANIELLE	What lady's that which doth enrich the hand
	Of yonder knight?
ANN	I know not, sir.
DANIELLE	O, she doth teach the torches to burn bright:
	It seems she hangs upon the cheek of night
	As a rich jewel in an Ethiop's ear:
	Beauty too rich for use, for earth too dear.

He crosses to get a closer look; Tybalt has overheard

TARA	This, by his voice, should be a Montague.
	(to the servant) Fetch me my rapier, boy; what dares the slave
	Come hither?
NATASHA	Why, how now, kinsman, wherefore storm you so?
TARA	Uncle, this is a Montague, our foe:
	A villain that is hither come in spite
	To scorn at our solemnity this night.
NATASHA	Young Romeo, is it?
TARA	'Tis he, that villain Romeo.
NATASHA	Content thee, gentle coz, let him alone.
	I would not for the wealth of all this town
	Here in my house do him disparagement.
	Therefore be patient and put off these frowns,
	An ill-beseeming semblance for a feast.
TARA	It fits when such a villain is a guest.
	I'll not endure him.
NATASHA	He shall be endured.
	What, Goodman boy, I say he shall; go to,
	Am I the master here, or you? Go to.

TARA	Why, uncle, 'tis a shame.
NATASHA	Go to, go to,
	You are a saucy boy, is't so indeed?
	Be quiet, or more light, more light for shame,
	I'll make you quiet. *(moving towards the other guests)*
	What, cheerly, my hearts.
TARA	Patience perforce, with wilful choler meeting,
	Makes my flesh tremble in their different greeting;
	I will withdraw, but this intrusion shall,
	Now seeming sweet, convert to bitterest gall.

Tybalt moves away upstage

DANIELLE	*(speaking to an imaginary Juliet)*
	If I profane with my unworthiest hand
	This holy shrine, the gentle sin is this:
	My lips two blushing pilgrims ready stand,
	To smooth the rough touch with a gentle kiss -

(breaking off and turning towards the auditorium) Oh, for heavens' sake, Neil, this is impossible!

The music suddenly stops

How can I act all smitten if there's no one here to be smitten by?

NEIL *(from the auditorium)* I know it's difficult, Danielle, but if you really concentrate and imagine she's there the words will come out all right... truthfully, I mean.

CLAIRE Truthfully, Neil, she's never here, so why don't we all imagine we're here and then we needn't rehearse the stupid play at all.

TARA Yeah, Neil, then we can all go down the pub and rehearse something worthwhile instead of trying to make sense of something written thousands of years ago.

NEIL *(coming up onto the stage and calling into the wings)* Can we kill the lights and have the workers on, please, Jamie? Don't show your ignorance, Tara, it was only written a few hundred years ago.

TARA Yeah, right, so that makes it bang up to date, then, doesn't it?

NEIL The story - the basic situation - is bang up to date, Tara. People are always going to fall in love with each other...

DAISY That's right - I'm always falling in and out of love with somebody or other!

AMY Usually the other, isn't it, Daisy?

DAISY Get lost! What would you know about it, anyway?

The stage lights fade out to black; general groans directed at Jamie, the technician. Working lights snap up

JAMIE *(entering from the wings)* Sorry, Neil, couldn't find the switch in the dark for a moment.

NATASHA This isn't really getting us anywhere, Neil, is it? We're behind schedule as it is, and this is the third rehearsal running that Sarah's not been here. I think the play could be really good -

AMY Good for nothing, you mean.

NEIL All right! I'll 'phone her and see when she's going to get here. While I'm doing that, it might be a good idea if you were to go through the first part of that scene again - it was all a bit lifeless. Remember, this is supposed to be a party - you're all enjoying yourselves.

CLAIRE I don't think our acting's good enough for that, Neil.

DAISY Speak for yourself - I'm a marvellous actress!

NEIL I'll be back in a minute. *(calling across the stage)* Lydia, can you give them a line to go from, please?

LYDIA *(coming forward slightly)* Where do you want them to go from, then?

NEIL I don't know - anywhere. You decide.

He disappears into the wings, pulling a mobile 'phone from his pocket. Lydia shrugs at the others and goes back to her seat. A few moments' silence

MEL I don't know why he's bothering to 'phone her - she's not really interested, is she?

DAISY Not in the play, no; but he thinks she's interested in him.

MEL Yeah, well, Neil's not really on the same planet as the rest of us, is he? Look at his ideas for this production.

ALEX Actually, I thought it was going really well. I think Neil's exaggerating a bit about that scene. And the costumes look pretty good. I know there's a bit more to do on some of them, but under the lights they look...

MEL Well, we think the whole thing's a bit silly, really, don't we, Ann?

ANN I don't know, it's...

MEL I mean, an all-girl Romeo and Juliet - it's a bit weird, I think. And Ann does, too, don't you, Ann?

ANN Well, I don't know about...

MEL So I think you'd have trouble making it truthful, Danielle, even if Sarah ever did turn up, because you're a girl and she's a girl and...

DANIELLE Put a sock in it, Mel, you're giving me a headache.

MEL Sorry I spoke, but it all seems a bit pointless to me. And what's the idea of all this black and white - not exactly subtle, is it?

NATASHA I think Neil's trying to focus on the characters and their relationships, so he doesn't want any extraneous distractions -

AMY Like you, Mel.

DAISY Any what distractions, Natasha?

NATASHA Extraneous, you know, unnecessary, beside the point. And he sees the story as timeless, not belonging to any particular period, so it's irrelevant when it was written.

ALEX And I think Neil thinks having all girls will show the play's universal - it could happen to anyone, anywhere.

NATASHA That's right, Alex. It's a story for all time.

CLAIRE Well, we're going to need an eternity if we're ever going to get it ready. And we'll never do that without a Juliet.

DANIELLE Perhaps someone else should take over the part.

TARA Who? We're all doing something already.

AMY I know - what about Jamie doing it!

DAISY Yeah, that's sensible, Amy; then we'd have a female Romeo and a male Juliet - and that would be weird!

JAMIE I can't do it, anyway - I've got all the lighting and sound to sort out.

AMY It was a joke - honestly, hasn't anyone got a sense of humour?

ALEX Well, we're not going to get much further without someone playing Juliet. What about somebody reading in until we can find someone to take over the part properly.

TARA Same argument - we're all doing something important already.

AMY Lydia isn't.

TARA She's the stage manager.

AMY Yeah, but she doesn't actually do anything, does she? Just sits in the corner with the script and watches. She doesn't even give you a prompt when you need one.

DAISY Like every other word in your case.

AMY Shut it, you.

JAMIE I think that's quite a good idea. She could still prompt - when necessary - because she'd have the book in her hand.

TARA Well, I suppose, if we're going to do the play, it would mean we could get on with rehearsals without having to stop every five minutes.

DANIELLE Hold on a minute - aren't we forgetting something?

DAISY Are we?

AMY Like what?

DANIELLE No one's actually asked Lydia what she thinks about the idea.

JAMIE Good point. Lydia, what do you think?

LYDIA I've never done any acting.

JAMIE Well, you wouldn't actually have to act, exactly - just read the lines on stage so that the others have someone to react to.

Lydia is not keen

TARA Yeah, come on, Lyd. You said you wanted to get involved in something.

LYDIA I am involved.

TARA I know, but you could get more involved, instead of just sitting over there without saying anything.

LYDIA I can't act.

DAISY It's easy! You just prance about saying the lines. *(she demonstrates)*

> O then I see Queen Mab hath been with you:
> She is the fairies' midwife, and she comes
> In shape no bigger than an agate-stone
> On the forefinger of an alderman,
> Drawn with a team of little atomies
> Over men's noses as they lie asleep:
> Her waggon-spokes -

AMY That's not acting - that's over-acting!

DAISY At least I bring it to life; not like you, waddling all over the stage like a great pudding!

AMY Yeah, well, the Nurse is supposed to be an old woman, isn't she?

DAISY An old woman, yes - not an old hippopotamus!

Amy gives Daisy the benefit of an appropriate gesture. Neil returns from the wings, making a show of putting his 'phone back in his pocket

MEL Here he comes - Mr Yuppie!
ANN Don't, Mel, he's doing his best.

Mel gives Ann a surprised look, as if to say 'Whose side are you on?"

NEIL Well, I managed to get hold of her -
DAISY In your dreams, Neil!
NEIL - and she says she's sorry she couldn't make it but something came up.
AMY In your dreams, Neil!

Amy and Daisy splutter with laughter

NATASHA OK, Neil, what did she say?
NEIL Well, the thing is, she missed the train.

Pause

DANIELLE Is that it? Why?
NEIL Why?
DANIELLE Why did she miss the train?
NEIL Oh, I see. Well, she was buying some shoes -
CLAIRE What!
NEIL Shoes. Well, she had to have them, you see, and by the time she'd got them, she'd missed the train.
CLAIRE I don't believe this.
NATASHA So why couldn't she get the next one? This is supposed to be a three hour rehearsal.
NEIL Yes, I know... *(he pauses uneasily)* I think she thought that by the time she got here it would be too late and we'd have finished and she'd have made a wasted journey, and so... you know... *(he dries up lamely)*.
CLAIRE For God's sake, Neil, if you weren't so pathetic -
NATASHA All right, Claire, I don't think that's going to get us anywhere. Neil, while you were 'phoning, we talked about getting someone to read in Juliet until we could find somebody else to take over the part.
NEIL But what about Sarah?

They stare at him without speaking

All right, all right. Maybe it would be better if someone else took over. But who? We haven't got anyone spare.
MEL *(to Daisy)* Except him! *(they giggle into their hands)*
NATASHA We talked about maybe Lydia reading in for the time being.
NEIL Lydia! But she's -
NATASHA Stage Manager. We know - and she's not very keen, anyway.
JAMIE But I'm sure she could do it. She's never really had the chance.

LYDIA I've never asked for the chance.

JAMIE But you don't know what you can do until you've tried. And it would only be temporary, until we can find someone else. One of us must know someone who could do it.

TARA Go on, Lydia, give it a go.

DANIELLE It would really be a big help to me, Lydia. I don't think I can go on talking to thin air much longer.

LYDIA *(to Danielle)* I can see it must be difficult for you.

DAISY *(hand on forehead)* So difficult, so difficult, I can't go on...

JAMIE Shut up, Daisy.

DANIELLE Go on, Lydia. Will you? Just for today, say, so that we can get on with the rehearsal. So's I've got someone to speak to.

LYDIA I wouldn't be able to put much feeling into it. Just say the lines... you know...

DANIELLE That's fine - it'd be better than no lines at all.

Pause. Everyone is looking at Lydia

LYDIA OK. I'll give it a go.

NEIL Great! Then we can get on. Let's carry on with the scene where we left off - Romeo and Juliet meeting for the first time. Positions, everyone, please. Jamie, can we have the stage lights again?

JAMIE You got it. *(he disappears into the wings)*

NEIL Lydia, you know where Juliet is supposed to be, don't you?

LYDIA I <u>was</u> watching what was happening, Neil.

NEIL Yeah, OK, OK.

The stage lights come on and the workers go off

We'll go from... *(looking at his script)* ...Romeo's line "If I profane," etc., etc. OK, Danielle?

DANIELLE Fine.

NEIL Ready, Lydia? Everyone else, quiet, please. Daisy, for heavens' sake, concentrate for once.

DAISY Sorry I breathed!

NEIL All right, Lydia?

Lydia nods

OK - action!

DANIELLE   If I profane with my unworthiest hand
                         This holy shrine, the gentle sin is this:
                         My lips two blushing pilgrims ready stand,
                         To smooth the rough touch with a gentle kiss.

Pause

NEIL Your line, Lydia...

LYDIA *(sharply)* I know!

She reads from the script, keeping her eyes glued to the page, with practically no attempt at expression or gesture

> Good pilgrim you do wrong your hand too much
> Which mannerly devotion shows in this,
> For saints have hands, that pilgrims' hands do touch,
> And palm to palm is holy palmer's kiss.

DANIELLE Have not saints lips and holy palmers too?
LYDIA Ay, pilgrim, lips that they must use in prayer.
DANIELLE *(doing her best to keep it going)*
> O then, dear saint, let lips do what hands do;
> They pray, grant thou, lest faith turn to despair.

LYDIA Saints do not move, though grant for prayers' sake.
DANIELLE Then move not while my prayer's effect I take...

There is an awkward silence

NEIL Carry on.
DANIELLE This is where we're supposed to kiss.

There are muffled snorts and giggles from Amy and Daisy

NATASHA Grow up, you two, for goodness' sake.
DANIELLE What do you want to do here, Neil?
NEIL What were you going to do with Sarah?
AMY *(to Daisy)* I know what he'd like to do with Sarah.

More snorts and giggles

ALEX I don't know what you two are finding so funny...

Increased snorts and giggles from Amy and Daisy

... but this is supposed to be a tragedy, you know.
DAISY It's certainly a tragedy for Neil.

Amid uncontrollable snorting and giggling, Daisy and Amy exit

NEIL What had we blocked with Sarah, Danielle?
DANIELLE Nothing. She was never here long enough to get to this bit.
NEIL O - kay. I don't think we need anything particularly passionate at this point in the play. Just the merest contact will probably do.
DANIELLE Contact between what?
NEIL Between you and Juliet.
DANIELLE No - not who, what?
NEIL Oh, I see. Er... *(he seems confused and embarrassed)* well, can't you just use your imagination?
DANIELLE Well, we could - but I'm not sure how well it would suit the play.

CLAIRE I don't see why there has to be any contact - it could just be a token 'mmwwaah', couldn't it?

LYDIA Do we have to do anything?

NEIL Sorry?

LYDIA Why do we have to do anything?

TARA It's in the script, Lydia - they're supposed to kiss.

LYDIA But it's not actually going to be me, is it? So why do we need to do anything... why do I need to do anything?

JAMIE There's no point in putting the cart before the horse, is there, Neil? I mean, Lydia's only agreed to read in for the time being and it's the first time she's done it.

NATASHA It's the first time she's done anything like this.

ALEX Yes, it's not fair to push her too hard straight away.

NEIL All right, all right. Never mind that we're about three weeks behind schedule. Never mind that I've got a leading lady who's never here. Never mind that half the cast seem to think the whole thing's a joke, and the other half are so casual they'd make a pair of slippers seem energetic.

JAMIE That's not exactly fair, Neil, is it? Some of us have been committed to the project right from the start.

NATASHA That's right - and precious little thanks we get for it.

NEIL OK - I'm sorry. Things are beginning to get to me. Let's try the passage leading up to the kiss again. And Lydia, if you could put a bit more feeling into it, it would be a help.

LYDIA I'm doing my best.

NEIL I know, but Danielle really needs a bit more feedback from you.

CLAIRE Sounds like a request for the impossible, if you ask me.

DANIELLE Shut up, Claire. It's not easy for Lydia.

CLAIRE Oh, I'm so sorry. Just pretend I'm not here, all right?

NEIL Let's go from Romeo: "Have not saints lips..." When you're ready.

DANIELLE   Have not saints lips and holy palmers too?

LYDIA   *(as wooden as before)*
Ay pilgrim, lips that they must use in prayer.

DANIELLE   *(trying too hard)*
O then, dear saint, let lips do what hands do,
They pray, grant thou, lest faith turn to despair.

LYDIA   *(beginning to struggle)*
Saints do not move, though grant for prayers' sake.

DANIELLE   Then move not while my prayer's effect I take.

Lydia suddenly breaks away

NEIL Move not, it says, Lydia. How can you kiss each other if you're half a mile apart?

LYDIA I don't want to kiss her.

NEIL But it's part of the action. We can't play the scene properly if you don't.

LYDIA I didn't want to play the scene at all. You all forced me into it.

CLAIRE Oh, I see, we threatened you, did we? Advanced on you chanting menacingly, did we?

DANIELLE Lay off, Claire.

NATASHA Leave her alone, Claire. You're not being fair.

CLAIRE What's being fair got to do with it? She can't act. She makes the words sound like a foreign language. She won't even look at Romeo- it's useless.

LYDIA I'm doing my best.

CLAIRE Well, your best isn't good enough, is it?

DANIELLE Claire, will you just shut up. You're not helping.

NEIL Girls, I...

DANIELLE Stay out of this, Neil. It's got nothing to do with you.

NEIL I'm sorry?

CLAIRE Why don't we just call the whole thing off? There's no point trying to do 'Romeo and Juliet' with a Juliet who makes Lady Penelope look like a graduate of RADA.

LYDIA Shut up! Just shut up, can't you, you bitch.

DANIELLE Lydia -

LYDIA I wish I'd never come. *(to Tara)* I just wish you'd never persuaded me to come.

TARA But I thought -

LYDIA Leave me alone. Just leave me alone, can't you...leave... me... alone! *(rushes out)*

DANIELLE Why did you have to say all that?

CLAIRE Well it's true, isn't it?

DANIELLE Claire, I can't believe sometimes how insensitive you are.

CLAIRE Well, if being sensitive means shutting your eyes to things, I'm not sorry I'm not! *(stalks away)*

TARA Great. Now what do we do?

ANN Excuse me. Neil.

NEIL Yes, what do you want?

ANN I'm sorry, only...

NEIL Oh, Ann. No, I'm sorry, I didn't realise you were there. No, sorry, what I mean is, I didn't know it was you... sorry, I meant...

JAMIE I should keep quiet, Neil, before the hole gets any bigger.

NEIL Yes. OK. What is it, Ann?

ANN It's just that Mel and I are supposed to be doing props., only we don't know what you want yet. Do we, Mel?

MEL No. Are you feeling all right?

ANN Me? Why?

MEL You said more than two words.

ANN I'm allowed, aren't I? I don't usually get much of a chance with you rabbiting on.

NEIL That's a very helpful suggestion, Ann. Perhaps this would be a good opportunity to talk about the technical side of things. Alex, Jamie, would you join us? I could do with a coffee, anyway. Let's go in the green room.

ALEX I've got some more drawings I'd like you to look at, Neil... some ideas for the bedroom scene.

NEIL As long as it's all black and white - fine.

TARA Neil. Any chance of doing the fight scene? We've hardly looked at it.

NEIL Sure, Tara. We'll do that next. Is that OK with you, Danielle?

DANIELLE What's that?

NEIL Tara would like to do the fight scene in a minute.

DANIELLE Fine with me. But we'll have to find Daisy.

NEIL Well, we're just going to have a coffee and chat about technical thingys.

TARA I'll go and look for the irrepressible Daisy - I'm quite looking forward to running my sword through her!

NEIL OK. Let's aim to be back here in ten minutes or so.

TARA See you later, then.

Everyone except Danielle and Claire exits. A pause

DANIELLE I don't know why you have to get so worked up. It's just a play.

CLAIRE Yes, and plays need people who can act.

DANIELLE She's just standing in. And I think if you and the others were to give her half a chance, she'd surprise us all.

CLAIRE Whose side are you on, anyway? I thought we were supposed to be friends.

DANIELLE I am your friend.

CLAIRE And Lydia?

DANIELLE I hardly know Lydia.

CLAIRE But you'd like to know her better, is that it?

DANIELLE Claire, you're being totally unreasonable. I just think she should be given more leeway, that's all.

CLAIRE Well, you can give her all the leeway you like. I'm going for a coffee.

DANIELLE Claire...

But Claire has gone. Danielle is lost in thought for a few moments, then rouses herself and begins to rehearse some lines

> He jests at scars that never felt a wound.
> *(to herself)* That's true enough.

Unnoticed by Danielle, Lydia enters upstage and stands watching her

> But soft, what light through yonder window breaks?
> It is the east, and Juliet is the sun.
> It is my lady, O it is my love,
> O that she knew she were.
> See how she leans her cheek upon her hand.

Lydia does so

> O that I were a glove upon that hand,
> That I might touch that cheek.

LYDIA   O Romeo, Romeo, wherefore art thou Romeo?

DANIELLE *(startled)* Lydia - I didn't know... you said that without the script.

LYDIA It's the only bit I can do from memory. Not difficult to remember that line.

DANIELLE You said it right, too.

LYDIA What do you mean?

DANIELLE Most people say the line as if 'wherefore?' meant 'where?'. But it doesn't - it means 'why?'.

LYDIA Isn't that obvious?

DANIELLE It doesn't seem to be to most people. *(pause)* It wasn't to Sarah.

LYDIA Oh. *(pause)* I'm sorry I stormed out just now. They... things were just getting to me... you know.

DANIELLE I don't blame you. In fact, I wouldn't have blamed you if you hadn't come back.

LYDIA I know I'm not very good. But I've never done anything like this before. I've never really had the chance. No one at home is interested in this sort of thing, really. I almost didn't come at all. But Tara practically dragged me here.

DANIELLE Yes, she can be quite persuasive, in a physical sort of way.

LYDIA But I've really enjoyed watching the rehearsals. I didn't know the play at all - I mean, I knew the basic story, but not the details. I think it's great. And actually, I think Neil is right about it being an always story.

DANIELLE An always story?

LYDIA Yes. I mean, it doesn't matter when or where it's happening. It's about something deep down that'll always be there.

DANIELLE Love, you mean.

LYDIA Yes, but other things, as well. Like families and friendship. *(pause)* It's not a good idea for families to quarrel.

DANIELLE *(thoughtfully)* Or friends...

LYDIA It doesn't do any good in the end.

DANIELLE No, it doesn't. Especially when the quarrel is over something silly.

Pause

You're quite surprising, really.

LYDIA Am I?

DANIELLE All this time you've been sat at that table, hardly saying a word, and now here you are coming out with all this.

LYDIA Well, there've been plenty of others talking.

DANIELLE Yes, but mostly it's just hot air. In the case of Amy and Daisy, it's <u>always</u> hot air!

LYDIA Anyway, I think the play could be really good. *(pause)* You're really good. I'm sorry I wasn't. In that scene. I know I wasn't giving you anything... any help, I mean.

DANIELLE You were giving me more than I got from Sarah - dialogue! *(pause)* Look - why don't we try it again? Just the two of us. It'll be easier for you with no one else here.

LYDIA I don't know. I don't know if it'll make any difference. I'm not really very good.

DANIELLE That's not what I told Claire just now.

LYDIA What do you mean?

DANIELLE I told her I thought you could surprise us all - so I'd better give you a chance to prove me right. Or perhaps you'd better give me a chance to prove me right! Let's go from where they first meet... "If I profane with my unworthiest hand". OK?

LYDIA OK. I'll try. But don't expect too much.

DANIELLE Just let the words do the work for you. Try it without looking at the script. I bet you know more of it than you think. Romeo and Juliet have been drawn to each other across the dance floor. It's as if everyone else has faded into the background, and it's just them, like they're the only two people in the world. So they're facing each other, just them, no one else, totally alone and caught up in each other's presence. Romeo takes Juliet's hands - I take your hands - like this. Ready?

Lydia nods

DANIELLE   If I profane with my unworthiest hand
                          This holy shrine, the gentle sin is this,
                          My lips two blushing pilgrims stand,
                          To smooth the rough touch with a gentle kiss.
Now he kisses her hand - I kiss your hand - like this... (*she does*) Now Juliet speaks
- try to keep looking at me the whole time. I'll prompt you - I ought to know it - I've
done it enough times at home.

LYDIA   Good pilgrim, you do...
DANIELLE   Wrong..
LYDIA   ...wrong your hand too much,
                          Which mannerly devotion shows in this,
                          For...
DANIELLE   ...saints have hands
LYDIA   For saints have hands, that pilgrims' hands do touch,
                          And palm to palm...
DANIELLE Now we touch palms, like this...
LYDIA   ...palm to palm is holy palmers' kiss.
DANIELLE   Have not saints lips and holy palmers too?
LYDIA   Ay, pilgrim, lips that they must use in prayer.
DANIELLE   O then, dear saint, let lips do what hands do,
                          They pray, grant thou, lest faith turn to despair.

Pause

DANIELLE (*prompting*) Saints do not...
LYDIA   Saints do not move, though grant for prayers' sake.
DANIELLE (*quite slowly*)
                          Then move not while my prayer's effect I take.

*They are looking into each other's eyes. Long pause. Mel and Amy appear upstage,
stop suddenly when they see Danielle and Lydia. After a moment, Amy giggles
quietly. Danielle and Lydia release hands and move apart*

DANIELLE That was very good. I felt... it felt as if there was...
LYDIA Yes. Me too.
DANIELLE Your words were great - I think you've been secretly learning them on the
sly.
LYDIA No. I just seemed to know them - well, nearly.
DANIELLE Looks like the others are coming back. Let's go outside and go through the
words again before we do the fight scene.
LYDIA OK.
DANIELLE (*to Mel and Amy*) Tell Neil I'll be back in a minute, will you?
AMY All right.
MEL Don't worry - we'll tell him.

Lydia and Danielle exit upstage, just as Claire returns from the other side and sees them go

MEL They seem to have hit it off all right.

CLAIRE What do you mean?

AMY Rehearsing that lovey-dovey bit all alone like that.

MEL Of course, you have to really feel something for each other if you're going to act a scene like that, don't you?

CLAIRE Shut up, Mel.

AMY But, of course, Lydia's only reading in, isn't she?

MEL Didn't look as though she was doing much reading to me.

AMY Probably can't read much, anyway, coming from where she comes from.

CLAIRE Where's that, then?

AMY You know, her family. Dad in prison, mother on the bottle, all that.

MEL Don't think she ever went to school very much, what with having to look after the little brothers.

CLAIRE You're making it up.

AMY Would we? Well, yes, we might. But, as it happens, we're not.

MEL My mum works at the police station. She gets to know about all that sort of thing.

CLAIRE And, of course, she comes straight home and tells you all about it.

MEL No. But I've got ears. I hear her telling dad.

AMY So it's not surprising poor little Lydia is socially deprived.

MEL And it's equally not surprising that she'd get pally with the first person offering her a shoulder to cry on.

AMY In this case, Danielle.

MEL Looks like you're out in the cold, Claire.

CLAIRE You think so? We'll see.

Neil and the others come back in. He is all bustle

NEIL OK - we're going to rehearse the first part of the fight scene, up to the killing of Mercutio. Is everyone here?

ALEX Danielle's not here at the moment, Neil - she's rehearsing with Lydia, I think.

NEIL Oh, right. Well, we'll need her for this - could someone fetch her?

NATASHA I'll get her, Neil.

NEIL Thanks, Natasha.

Natasha exits

CLAIRE Neil, could I have a word?

NEIL Yes, sure.

CLAIRE A private word?

NEIL Private - *(he looks alarmed)* - yes, OK.

They move downstage away from the others, who are preparing for the fight

CLAIRE What have you decided about Lydia?

NEIL About Lydia? What do you mean?

CLAIRE Are you going to let her play Juliet?

NEIL Well, I...

CLAIRE Because, frankly, I don't think it would be a very good idea.

NEIL Not a...

CLAIRE I mean, she's got no experience. You saw how she performed - or rather didn't - in that scene with Danielle. She's hopeless.

NEIL Well, I agree she needs some coaching, but...

CLAIRE And how do we know she's reliable, you know, with her background?

NEIL Background?

CLAIRE Yeah, you know, at home.

NEIL No, actually, Claire, I don't know. And I've got enough problems without you giving me any more.

CLAIRE I just think you should be careful, that's all.

NEIL Yes, well, I will be... now I'd better get on with the rehearsal, or we're never going to get this show ready.

CLAIRE Don't say I didn't warn you.

Neil turns to the others and calls out; Claire moves to one side, half smiling to herself

NEIL OK - the fight: Act Three, Scene One. Everyone here?

JAMIE No sign of Danielle yet. *(calling off)* Danielle!

Some of the others join in with a chorus of 'Danielle!'. She runs onstage

DANIELLE All right - here I am. Sorry to keep you waiting, Neil. I was just going through some lines with Lydia.

CLAIRE Hope you had your dictionary with you, then.

DANIELLE Don't be so...

NEIL OK - can we get on, please? We'll go from Romeo's entrance - Tybalt's line: "Well, peace be with you..." Tara, Daisy - are you ready? Remember to just walk through the fight part so that no one gets hurt.

TARA *(jumping up and down energetically)* I'm ready.

DAISY I will not budge for no man's pleasure, I.

NEIL Well, you'd better budge, or we can't start the scene.

DAISY No - that's my line; it's the cue for Romeo's entrance: I will not budge...

NEIL *(consulting his script)* Oh, yes; sorry. Off you go, then. You others, you're the crowd in this scene, so let's have some decent reactions, OK?

They take up positions and the scene begins

DAISY I will not budge for no man's pleasure, I.

TARA Well, peace be with you sir, here comes my man.

DAISY But I'll be hanged, sir, if he wear your livery.

NATASHA *(interrupting)* Neil - that line doesn't really make sense if we're all wearing black and white anyway, does it?

NEIL Well, no, not literally - but we're asking the audience to use their imaginations a bit. They've got to do a bit of work as well.

ALEX I could add something if you think it's necessary, Neil.

NEIL No - it isn't necessary. Carry on, please.

TARA Romeo, the love I bear thee can afford
No better term than this: thou art a villain.

DANIELLE Tybalt, the reason that I have to love thee
Doth much excuse the...

NEIL *(interrupting)* Danielle - don't forget that Romeo's attitude to the Capulets is different now -

CLAIRE You can say that again!

NEIL ...he's fallen in love with Juliet, so he's not as aggressive with Tybalt as he used to be.

DANIELLE OK... doth much excuse the appertaining rage
To such a greeting; villain am I none.
Therefore farewell, I see'st thou know'st me not.

TARA Boy, this shall not excuse the injuries
That thou hast done me, therefore turn and draw.

NEIL OK - now Tybalt is getting really worked up. And the rest of you - the crowd - you should be sensing a fight brewing - there's a growing sense of excitement.

AMY *(yawning)* Oh, this is <u>so</u> exciting!

NATASHA Shut up, Amy; act your age for once.

NEIL Carry on, Danielle.

DANIELLE I do... I do... sorry, Neil, I've forgotten the line.

NEIL *(turning to the corner)* Prompt, please, Lydia - oh.

CLAIRE Never there when you need her, is she, Neil? Unless, of course, you're Danielle.

DANIELLE Don't be so pathetic, Claire.

NEIL Can someone else go on the book, please?

ALEX I'll do it.

NEIL Thanks, Alex. Now can we get on?

ALEX Protest, Danielle.

DANIELLE What about?

ALEX No - I do protest - that's the line.

DANIELLE Oh yes. I do protest -

CLAIRE Me too.

DANIELLE *(ignoring her)* I never injured thee,
But love thee better than thou canst devise.

Pause

ALEX Daisy, it's your line.

DAISY Oh, sorry - I wasn't concentrating.

TARA What a surprise.

DAISY Well, it's difficult with all this stopping and starting. *(pause)* What is the line?

ALEX O calm..

DAISY O calm, dishonourable, vile submission.
Tybalt, you rat-catcher, will you walk?

TARA   What wouldst thou have with me?
DAISY   Good King of Cats, nothing but one of your nine lives.
TARA   I am for you.
DANIELLE   Gentle Mercutio, put thy rapier up.
DAISY   Come, sir.

She flies at Tara with her sword swirling

NEIL Steady, Daisy- stay in control.

There is some fairly wild clashing of swords

DANIELLE   Gentlemen, for shame, forbear this outrage.
              Hold Tybalt, good Mercutio.

Mercutio is wounded by Tybalt, thanks to Romeo's intervention

DAISY   *(staggering about all over the stage)* I am hurt:
              A plague o' both your houses, I am sped:
              Is he gone and hath nothing?

Tara is still there; Daisy looks at her meaningfully

              Is he gone and hath nothing?
TARA Oh - sorry.

*She rushes off to one side; Daisy dies melodramatically. There is spontaneous
applause from some of the others*

NEIL Thank you so much, Daisy. Wonderful, just wonderful. Forgetting for a moment
that your death was just a little bit over the top, Mercutio is supposed to die <u>offstage</u>.
DAISY I think that's a wasted opportunity!
NEIL However, apart from the fact that the scene took about ten times longer than it
should have done and not everyone knows their lines and Mercutio's death needs a
bit more work - that wasn't at all bad!
TARA Neil - I've just had a thought!
NEIL All right - I know it wasn't perfect, but I think we're making progress.
TARA No, not about the scene. About who could play Juliet. I've got a friend who's just
moved back into the area. She's been in lots of things. I'm sure she'd be able to do it.
DANIELLE What about Lydia?
CLAIRE Who?
JAMIE Come on, Tara - Lydia's working on the lines now.
ALEX I've heard her - she's beginning to sound quite good.
CLAIRE But she doesn't have any experience, though, does she?
AMY No acting experience at all!
JAMIE Well, you'd certainly know about that, wouldn't you, Amy?
AMY and MEL Oooohhh!!
TARA What about it, Neil? I could give her a call.

DANIELLE Hang on, Neil. I thought we were going to give Lydia a chance.

CLAIRE She's had her chance, hasn't she. And she was crap.

DANIELLE She was nervous.

CLAIRE OK. She was nervous and crap.

TARA Neil...?

NEIL Well, I suppose it wouldn't do any harm to ask... keep our options open. The thing is, we don't have very long - at least Lydia already has some idea of what we're doing - you know, the style of the production, that sort of thing.

DANIELLE And she's already working on the lines.

CLAIRE Yeah, maybe she is at the moment, but she won't be able to do much with them when she gets home, will she?

JAMIE What do you mean?

CLAIRE Well, you know, with all the problems there...

JAMIE I really don't know what you're talking about, Claire.

AMY and **MEL** We do!

JAMIE Shut up.

TARA Neil - shall I ring Vicky or what?

NEIL Vicky?

TARA My friend.

NEIL Yes, OK, go ahead, I'll...

He is interrupted by the ringing of his mobile 'phone. He digs it out of his pocket

Yes, hello... oh, hi.... yes, we're still rehearsing. *(to the others)* It's Sarah. *(back to the 'phone)* Well, the rate we're going at the moment, we're going to be here until the weekend... well, I don't know, we were sort of thinking of alternatives... I know you're supposed to be playing the part, but actually the others are getting a bit, you know...

DAISY Pissed off!

NEIL ...uneasy about you never being here... well, all right, not never, but not often. *(to the others)* She wants to know if she can carry on. *(general groans. To the 'phone)* What, Sarah... I can't hear you... *(to the others)* shut up a minute... *(to the 'phone)* Well, all right... get here as soon as you can. *(he puts the 'phone back in his pocket. rather lamely)* She's going to get here as soon as she can.

DANIELLE Great!

NEIL What?

DANIELLE Wonderful! So what about Lydia? We get her to take on the part...

CLAIRE She was only reading in, wasn't she. And I say 'reading' with some hesitation.

DANIELLE Originally, yes. But she's really into it now. And she's good - she could be really good. Alex heard her.

ALEX Yes - I think she's doing really well.

CLAIRE What's the real reason you want Lydia to play the part, Danielle?

DANIELLE What do you mean, the real reason?

CLAIRE You know what I mean.

DANIELLE Do I?

AMY We think you do, don't we, Mel?

MEL We certainly do.

DANIELLE I don't know what you're talking about.

AMY It's not natural, really, is it?

ALEX What isn't?

MEL Oh, for heavens' sake, Alex, you'd have to be blind.

JAMIE This is getting us nowhere. Neil, why don't you speak to Lydia? Find out how she really feels about the part. I think we owe it to her to give her a say in all this.

NEIL *(resignedly)* OK. I'll have a chat with her. Where is she?

ANN She was in the green room a little while ago. Shall I fetch her, Neil?

NEIL Yes, thanks, Ann.

Ann goes out

Now can the rest of you go outside and go through the fight scene again. Jamie, could you take them through it?

JAMIE No problem.

NEIL And Daisy - no melodramatics this time, OK?

DAISY OK - if you say so. But I feel I'm hiding my light under a bushel, or whatever it is.

TARA Best place for it.

NEIL Go!

DAISY We're going!

She leads the others out, performing her dying act as she goes. Danielle, watched by Claire, hangs back briefly

DANIELLE Keep an open mind, Neil, won't you?

NEIL Yes, of course.

Danielle and Claire follow the others. Neil mutters to himself and runs his hands through his hair

An open mind! Some hopes!

Lydia appears upstage

LYDIA Ann says you'd like a word with me, Neil.

NEIL Lydia. Hi. *(pause)* How's it going?

LYDIA *(a trifle suspicious)* All right. I've sort of found I knew quite a lot of the words already. From following rehearsals, I suppose. I didn't realise how much had sunk in.

NEIL Yeah. Great. *(short pause)* Hey, maybe you know everyone's words - you could be a kind of universal understudy!

He attempts a halfhearted laugh; Lydia does not join in

LYDIA I sort of got the feeling you'd like me to take over as Juliet.

NEIL Yes, well... it was good of you to read in like that at short notice. No notice, really. Danielle found it a great help, you know.

LYDIA I know. She told me. *(pause)* The thing is, Neil, I've really begun to get into it. I didn't think I could ever do anything like this. I didn't want to come, but Tara... you know. Anyway, I'm really enjoying it - I seem to understand what Juliet is feeling, you know? And Danielle has been... well, terrific, really. Really helpful and... supportive. *(pause)* So I suppose what I'm really trying to say is - if you'd like me to, I'd really like to carry on and play the part... if you'd like me to.

Short pause

NEIL Hey, who wanted to have a word with who?
LYDIA Sorry.
NEIL It's OK.

Pause

Look, Lydia...
LYDIA *(hurriedly)* I know I wasn't very good first time, when I read with Danielle, but I was nervous, not very confident... you know. But now I feel as though I know what I'm doing. I went through it again with Danielle and it really seemed to... go well... much better, anyway... not that that would be difficult, suppose.
NEIL No. *(hastily)* Sorry, I didn't mean...
LYDIA It's all right. I know what they're saying about me.
NEIL Not all of them. Only the silly <u>little</u> girls. *(pause)* Only the thing is, Lydia, Tara's got this friend - she's done quite a lot, apparently... of acting, and Tara thought that maybe she could ask her... And I just got this 'phone call from Sarah, would you believe?... and she's really sorry for missing so many rehearsals, but she'd really like to carry on and she won't miss any more so really what seems to be happening is...
LYDIA So you don't want me.
NEIL Well, no, it's not that, exactly, it's just...
LYDIA You've had a better offer - two better offers, in fact.
NEIL No. Well, yes - no, that didn't sound right. It's just that some of the others are worried that you might find a big part like Juliet difficult, you know, what with problems at home and everything...
LYDIA I beg your pardon?
NEIL Well, they said...
LYDIA Who said?
NEIL The others.
LYDIA Which others?
NEIL Well, Claire and Mel... Daisy...
LYDIA Said what?
NEIL That things weren't too good at home... your dad being in... it must be really difficult for you...
LYDIA And what do you think you know about it? Just because a couple of jealous little cats say something you take it on board just like that. You're pathetic, Neil.
NEIL Hold on a mo...
LYDIA You've got no idea how hard it was for me even to come here, let alone stand up in front of a lot of idiots like you and try something I've never even thought about doing before. OK. So I wasn't that good. But I was doing you a favour. You and your

precious play. You think - you all think - you're so much better than me, don't you? Poor little Lydia. She hasn't had the same chances as the rest of us. Poor deprived little Lydia. We don't want her pushing in where she doesn't know what's going on and isn't wanted anyway.

NEIL Lydia.

LYDIA Forget it, Neil. Where's that bitch Claire? I've got a few things to say to her as well.

She storms offstage; Neil follows her. The stage remains empty for a few moments, and then voices are heard from the wings; Mel, Daisy and Amy prance on

MEL Honestly, Dais, you should have seen them!

AMY Talk about eyes locked together! It was weird.

MEL *(overacting like mad)* My lips two blushing pilgrims ready stand,
To smooth the rough touch with a gentle kiss.

AMY *(exaggerating Lydia's original woodenness)* Ay Pilgrim, lips that you must use in prayer.

DAISY No, that's wrong. You looked at her!

AMY Sorry. *(bending over and looking at Mel's feet)* Saints do not move, though grant for... something's sake.

DAISY *(saying it wrong)* Romeo, Romeo, wherefore art thou, Romeo?

MEL But the second time they were like glue.

AMY Yeah, when they thought no one was watching. It was - you know - creepy. Like Danielle really was a guy.

DAISY Maybe she fancies herself as Leonardo di Caprio.

MEL Maybe Lydia fancies her as Leonardo di Caprio.

Brief pause

AMY Maybe Lydia fancies her as - her.

The others look at her

DAISY Uuugh! That makes me go all goose-fleshy.

MEL Yes, me too. But it was a bit like that.

DAISY You're not serious?

MEL I don't know. No. They couldn't. It's not, well, you know...

AMY It's not natural, you mean.

MEL But then, with a family like hers, probably anything goes.

AMY I bet they're at it all the time in her house.

MEL Bound to rub off, isn't it?

DAISY Yes, I suppose... *(pause)* Is Neil going to let her do it?

AMY Juliet?

DAISY Yeah.

MEL Dunno. Trouble with him is, he can never make a decision about anything.

Ann and Alex come on from the wings

MEL Hey, Ann, what's going on out there. Are we rehearsing, or what?
ANN Lydia nearly had a punch-up with Claire. Jamie managed to calm them down. Well, calm Lydia down, anyway.
ALEX Claire was being her usual catty self.
DAISY What's happening about Juliet?
ALEX Don't know.
ANN I don't think Neil knows what to do now. He's got Sarah on at him to carry on with the part...
ALEX And he seems to be unable to refuse her anything.
ANN - and Tara's on at him to get her friend Vicky along.
ALEX And Danielle and Jamie are on at him to give Lydia another chance. Who'd be a director? I'll just stick to the costumes... much less complicated.
DAISY Yeah, with the costumes everything's either black or white, isn't it - no grey bits.
ALEX Ha, ha. Very funny, Daisy.
ANN Actually, I think we're all being a bit hard on Lydia. I mean, she's new to all this, isn't she?
AMY Yes, we were just saying how much she seems to be enjoying herself, weren't we, girls?
DAISY Romeo, Romeo, wherefore art thou, Romeo?
MEL Over here, sweetie!
DAISY Let me come to thee, my love.

Daisy and Mel go into a lavish embrace

ALEX I don't think you three could ever take anything seriously, could you?
DAISY But we are serious, aren't we, Mel?
MEL Passionately!
ANN Alex, could I help you with the costumes? I think Mel can manage props. without me.
ALEX Sure. I could do with some help.
DAISY Help! Help!
ALEX You need help all right - try a psychiatrist!
AMY and **MEL** Oooohh!

Neil enters briskly followed by Jamie, Natasha, Danielle, Lydia, Claire and Tara

NEIL All right, Tara. I've got the message, OK? If I want you to call your friend, I'll let you know.
TARA I'm only trying to help, Neil. I'm committed to this play, remember? Unlike some others we could mention.
NEIL Yes, I know. And I'm grateful. But I'd like to see Lydia do a bit more of the part. Let's try the scene with Lady Capulet -
CLAIRE Oh great!
NEIL Act Three Scene Five, just after Romeo's exit.
AMY Never mind, Danielle.

Danielle gives her a contemptuous look

NEIL Juliet - Lydia - you sit on this bench. Jamie - could we have the bench over here, please?

JAMIE Coming up.

NEIL Imagine it's your bed. It's the morning after your wedding night. Romeo has just left. Lady Capulet comes in from over there. Everyone else, please just sit down somewhere and keep quiet. OK - action!

As the scene progresses it becomes clear that Claire is making little attempt to bring her character to life; in fact, she seems increasingly hostile towards Lydia, almost as if she were aiming the lines at her personally. Lydia, on the other hand, plays the scene with a simple directness and sincerity quite different from her showing in the first scene with Romeo

CLAIRE	Ho, daughter, are you up?
LYDIA	Who is't that calls? It is my lady mother.
CLAIRE	Why, how now, Juliet?
LYDIA	Madam, I am not well.
CLAIRE	Evermore weeping for your cousin's death?
LYDIA	Yet let me weep, for such a feeling loss.
CLAIRE	So shall you feel the loss, but not the friend Which you weep for.
LYDIA	Feeling so the loss, I cannot choose but ever weep the friend.
CLAIRE	Well, girl, thou weep'st not so much for his death, As that the villain lives which slaughtered him.
LYDIA	What villain, madam?
CLAIRE	*(with particular vehemence)* That same villain Romeo.

She cannot resist a flickering glance towards Danielle

NEIL Claire, you're making her much too angry. That comes later in the scene. If you do it too soon, you'll spoil the effect later.

CLAIRE I'm so sorry, Neil. I was just trying to feel the character.

NATASHA Wrong character, then, Claire.

NEIL Carry on, please.

LYDIA	God pardon him; I do with all my heart: And yet no man like he doth grieve my heart.
CLAIRE	That is because the traitor murderer lives. Then weep no more, For he shall soon keep Tybalt company: And then I hope thou wilt be satisfied.
LYDIA	Indeed, I never shall be satisfied With Romeo till I behold him.
CLAIRE	*(with anything but joyfulness in her voice and manner)* Well, now I'll tell thee joyful tidings, girl. Early next Thursday morn, The County Paris at St Peter's church Shall happily make thee there a joyful bride.

LYDIA　　I will not marry yet, and when I do, I swear
　　　　　　It shall be Romeo.
CLAIRE　　*(very hostile)* Here comes your father.

Natasha scrambles to her feet. Claire begins to push Lydia fiercely

　　　　　　Tell him so yourself:
　　　　　　And see how he will take it at your hands.
NATASHA　　When the sun sets...
NEIL That's enough.
NATASHA Neil! I was just about to speak! That was my entrance!
NEIL Claire, what on earth do you think you're doing? That's not how we originally set this scene.
CLAIRE Well, this isn't the original Juliet, is it, so I thought I'd try something different.
JAMIE It didn't work.
CLAIRE It worked for me.
DANIELLE I think Claire's letting her personal feelings get in the way of her acting.
CLAIRE Ha! Look who's talking!
DANIELLE There was no need to push Lydia around like that.
CLAIRE Getting very protective all of a sudden, aren't we?
DANIELLE There's nothing in the play that says Lady Capulet gets violent with Juliet.
CLAIRE There's nothing in the play that says the girl playing Romeo should actually fall for the girl <u>playing</u> Juliet!

There is a sudden and heavy silence. The two girls are face to face. Then Danielle turns away

DANIELLE *(quietly)* That's not fair, Claire.

Pause. Danielle moves apart from the others

CLAIRE Oh, get lost!

She disappears into the wings. A longish silence

JAMIE Neil, perhaps it would be a good idea if we had a bit of a break. I think everyone's getting a bit worked up.
NEIL Yes, sure. Let's have a break. Take a break, everyone. Five minutes.

Short pause

TARA Coffee, anyone?

She exits. Gradually, everyone else except Neil and Jamie drift offstage. Danielle is the last to go. Longish pause

JAMIE Who'd be a director, eh?

NEIL What really gets me is knowing the play could be really good. Some of them are actually getting into the parts well - Danielle, for instance, and Natasha. Even the daft ones like Daisy and Amy will be fine once they get their concentration sorted out.

JAMIE Yeah, but we've only got a couple of weeks, not half way into the next millennium!

NEIL It's all this stopping and starting - and can you believe the bitchiness?

JAMIE Girls, Neil. It's part of their psyche.

NEIL And the uncertainty about Juliet. Honestly, it's a joke really. First I had a Juliet, then I didn't have one, and now it looks as though I've got three. I don't know what to do. *(pause)* What do you suggest?

JAMIE *(thoughtfully)* Well, let's narrow the odds a bit. You can rule out Tara's friend straight away. She's never been up for it really. The real problem is what to do about Lydia, now that it looks like Sarah's coming back.

NEIL Yeah - that's a big problem. Sarah was good as Juliet...

JAMIE When she was here.

NEIL All right - when she was here. But she says she won't miss any more rehearsals.

JAMIE And Lydia?

NEIL I don't know what to do about Lydia.

JAMIE She was pretty good in the scene with Lady Capulet.

NEIL Yes - she was.

JAMIE In spite of Claire.

NEIL I know.

Pause. Natasha enters

NATASHA Neil -

NEIL Oh, hi, Natasha.

NATASHA Sorry for interrupting. *(pause)* It's just that some of us... some of us think we ought to give Lydia one more chance to show that she can play Juliet.

NEIL But...

NATASHA All right - I know Sarah's on her way. But she's not exactly been reliable, has she? How do you know you can count on her this time?

JAMIE Natasha's right, Neil.

NEIL Yes, but...

NATASHA And don't listen to all that muck about her background.

NEIL But what if it's...

NATASHA True? Does it matter?

NEIL Well...

NATASHA What matters is having someone who can play the part and you know she's going to be there when you need her.

Neil seems undecided

JAMIE She's right, Neil.

Pause

NATASHA Go on, Neil. What have you got to lose? If it looks as though Lydia's not going to be able to handle it, then you've got Sarah. *(pause)* Only, if you <u>do</u> decide Lydia can have the part, you've got to tell Sarah straight away.

Unseen by the others, Danielle enters upstage and stands listening

NEIL *(ruefully)* I know.
JAMIE Well?
NEIL OK. We'll give Lydia one more go.
NATASHA Great!
NEIL We'll try her in the farewell scene - you know, the last time Romeo and Juliet see each other alive.
NATASHA I'll go and tell her.
JAMIE You'd better tell Danielle as well.
DANIELLE It's all right - I heard.

Natasha goes out

NEIL Is that all right, then, Danielle?
DANIELLE Yes, sure. So long as you can handle Sarah.
NEIL If necessary, you mean?
DANIELLE Yes - if necessary.
NEIL I just hope we can get this sorted, finally.
JAMIE Yes. Me too. *(pause)* Look, while we're waiting, could you just come and have a quick look at the lighting plot? There's one cue I'm not sure about - where you want it, exactly.
NEIL OK. Lead on.

They exit. Danielle stands in thought for a few moments, then Lydia rushes on

LYDIA Danielle! Natasha says they're going to let me have a go at the farewell scene.
DANIELLE Yes.
LYDIA Well, that's great, isn't it? I thought it went really well when we went through it in the green room. Didn't you?
DANIELLE Yes, it did.
LYDIA If I can do it like that again, I'm sure Neil will let me play the part.
DANIELLE Lydia, I think you've done really well, reading in Juliet -
LYDIA But it's more than just reading in now, isn't it?
DANIELLE I suppose.
LYDIA I'm really into the character now - her feelings, her thoughts - you know.
DANIELLE Yes.
LYDIA And it's all because of you. I couldn't have done it for anyone... with anyone else

Danielle is silent

You make it easy for me, you see. When I'm doing those scenes with you, I don't feel as if I'm acting at all. *(pause)* It all seems... right, somehow.

Danielle turns away slightly

You've felt it too, haven't you. *(pause)* I know you have, Danielle. It's not just me, is it? There is something...

DANIELLE Yes, I know. I did feel something. But it's just the part, just the play. It's not real, Lydia, is it? It's just make-believe. That's what theatre is - it's pretend. It's just not real.

LYDIA I don't believe that. Not deep down inside. Not about feelings like these.

DANIELLE They're the characters' feelings - not ours.

LYDIA Aren't they?

DANIELLE Look, Lydia, I think you've let yourself get caught up in the whole situation. It's all been too quick for you. You haven't had time to sort things out - you're getting the play mixed up with reality.

LYDIA *(very quietly and with great feeling)* No, I'm not, Danielle.

Short pause

DANIELLE It's only a story.

LYDIA It's an always story, remember?

They stand looking at each other, and then Danielle moves away briskly

DANIELLE They'll be here in a moment. We'd better get ready.

LYDIA I am ready. But I won't do it if you don't want me to.

DANIELLE It's not that I don't want you to, it's just... I think it would be better if things... if things... anyway, they're expecting us to do the farewell scene, aren't they? We'd better not disappoint them.

LYDIA No. Especially not Claire.

Pause. Voices are heard offstage as everyone else, except Ann, comes back in

NEIL OK. Are you ready, you two? Lydia, we'll just have a look at this scene, all right?

LYDIA *(absolutely in control)* That's fine, Neil.

ALEX Do you want the costumes any more today, Neil? Only Ann's started to pack them away.

NEIL No, Alex. That's OK. I've seen them under the lights, and they look marvellous. Right - Danielle, Lydia, let's begin. We'll go from the beginning of the scene. Let's see - *(he consults his script)* - yes, that's right. They're kneeling downstage facing each other. Amy - don't forget you have a bit in this scene.

AMY OK.

Danielle and Lydia kneel, facing each other, down centre

NEIL Everyone else - quiet, please. And - action.

The scene is played with great intensity by both girls, but Lydia especially seems completely caught up in it. As the scene progresses, the others, watching, become increasingly engrossed

LYDIA	Wilt thou be gone? It is not yet near day:
	It was the nightingale and not the lark
	That pierced the fearful hollow of thine ear.
DANIELLE	It was the lark, the herald of the morn:
	No nightingale.
	I must be gone and live, or stay and die.
LYDIA	Yond light is not daylight, I know it, I;
	Therefore, stay yet, thou needs not to be gone.

Amy steps forward as the Nurse

AMY	Madam.
LYDIA	Nurse.
AMY	Your lady mother is coming to your chamber,
	The day is broke, be wary, look about.

Amy steps back and joins the others

| DANIELLE | Farewell, farewell, one kiss and I'll descend. |

Almost as if in slow motion, they kiss and move apart

LYDIA	I must hear from thee every day in the hour,
	For in a minute there are many days.
DANIELLE	Farewell.
LYDIA	O, think'st thou we shall ever meet again?
DANIELLE	I doubt it not.
LYDIA	O God, I have an ill-divining soul;
	Methinks I see thee now
	As one dead in the bottom of a tomb.
DANIELLE	Adieu, adieu.

Danielle moves away, leaving Lydia alone in the centre of the stage

LYDIA	O Fortune, Fortune, All men call thee fickle.
	Be fickle, Fortune:
	For then I hope thou wilt not keep him long,
	But send him back.

She is fixed to the spot, her eyes filled with tears, quite still. Everyone else is absolutely motionless. A long silence, finally broken by Ann entering from the wings

ANN Neil...

Everyone except Lydia turns to look at her

ANN Neil - Sarah's here. She's waiting in the green room. Didn't know what kind of reception she'd get if she came straight in. I said I'd... *(she becomes aware of the atmosphere)* ...tell you.

Pause. All eyes turn to Neil. He seems undecided what to do. Then Claire makes a move towards the exit

CLAIRE Come on, everyone, Sarah's back. Let's give her a great big welcome!

General vocal agreement suddenly breaks out and there is a general move offstage. Neil starts to go, then turns towards Lydia, seems about to speak, but then abruptly turns and goes off with the others. Danielle has started to follow but lingers, looking at Lydia, who is still facing front, not looking at anyone

CLAIRE Danielle, are you coming?

Pause

Danielle!
DANIELLE Yes - coming.

One final look at Lydia, and then she exits with Claire. Only Lydia and Jamie are left. After a moment Lydia sinks to her knees. She is quietly sobbing

JAMIE Lydia...
LYDIA *(through her tears)* Farewell. God knows when we shall meet again...
JAMIE Lydia... I...
LYDIA *(becoming increasingly distraught but with great significance)*
            Go, get thee hence, for I will not away.
            What's here? A cup closed in my true love's hand?
            Poison, I see, hath been his timeless end:
            O churl, drunk all? And left no friendly drop
            To help me after? I will kiss thy lips -
            Haply some poison yet doth hang on them,
            To make me die with a restorative.
            Thy lips are warm...

She breaks down, sobbing. Jamie kneels beside her and puts his arms round her

JAMIE It's all right, Lydia. It'll be all right.
LYDIA *(barely able to speak)* Oh Jamie, Jamie... I thought...
JAMIE I know...
LYDIA I thought it could be... could be... an always story.
JAMIE Some stories aren't like that. Sometimes people just aren't ready for stories like that. Until it's too late. Like Romeo and Juliet. But you can't give up...
LYDIA I know.
JAMIE There's lots of stories waiting to be told... and you never know which ones will turn out to be for always. You just have to keep on looking... just keep looking...

He looks at her

JAMIE ...keep looking.

They sit, huddled together, quiet, still

The lights fade slowly

Notes On The Play

General Note. This play was originally written for a group of students as a drama festival production (and won the award for Best Original Play at the 1998 Woking Drama Festival) and the staging is very simple, both because of the constraints of festival work and the nature of the play itself - a rehearsal situation. The characters are predominantly young, with a possible age-range of, say, 15 to mid-twenties, although Neil can be older than this. However, if directors feel it could work outside this span, please feel free to make minor changes to the script, where appropriate, in order to facilitate this.

Period. Contemporary.

Time. The action of the play is continuous.

Costumes. At the beginning of the play, those characters who appear in the 'Romeo and Juliet' scene should wear black and white: male characters white top, black trousers, black mask; female characters - black top, white skirt, white mask; non-'Romeo and Juliet' characters can wear anything that might be worn to a rehearsal. The 'Romeo and Juliet' characters, except Danielle and Claire, change out of black and white after the general exit on page 10; Claire can change after her exit on page 10, and Danielle after her exit on page 13.

Setting. The play takes place on a bare stage, but it is useful to have a simple arrangement of rostra and steps to enable different levels to be used. The layout can be at the discretion of the director. The only furniture required is a table (for the stage manager - set on stage), two chairs and a bench.

Properties

On Stage: 2 or 3 rehearsal swords (bated foils are ideal).
Personal: Jamie: clipboard with technical notes and diagrams, pencil.
            Neil: 'Romeo and Juliet' script, mobile telephone.
            Lydia: 'Romeo and Juliet' script.
            Alex: costume designs, 'Romeo and Juliet' script.

Lighting

The lighting is not specific to any particular location, but serves to underline the atmosphere and events of the play.

Cue 1	Fade up on 'Romeo and Juliet' scene	page 1
Cue 2	Quick fade to BO	page 2
Cue 3	Snap up to working-light effect over whole stage	page 2
Cue 4	Crossfade to Danielle and Lydia	page 6
Cue 5	Crossfade to working-light effect.	page 9
	Neil: I'm sorry...	

Sound effects

There are many other fine one act plays in the
Jasper range

including

Gilly's Gem
HTV Award 'Best original play'
Sandy Taylor

One Down, Three Across
Winner, South West Playwriting Competition
'Best production' Bridgwater Festival
Mary Jackson

Holmes Sweet Holmes
'A great success - a triumph' Edwin Parks - Journalist
'A machine built to arouse laughter' Colin Pinney - Festival Adjudicator
Jim Sperinck

Guess Who's Coming To Tea etc.'
Three prize-winning plays
Sandy Taylor

Two Little Dicky Birds etc.
Three plays 'Beautifully written piece of theatre', Playgoer
Sandy Taylor

Holiday Snaps
five one-act plays
Jim Sperinck

Free catalogue of all our plays, musicals and pantomimes

Jasper Publishing Ltd
115 Harlestone Road, Northampton NN5 7AQ
Tel: 01604 590315 Fax: 01604 591077